Latest Releases fr

AI for Smart Kids Ages 6-9: Discover How Artificial
Intelligence is Changing the World© 2023 by Dr. Leo Lexicon

AI FOR SMART KIDS AGES 6-9

Discover How Artificial Intelligence is
Changing the World

DR. LEO LEXICON

AI FOR SMART KIDS AGES 6-9
Discover how Artificial Intelligence is Changing the World

"AI for Smart Kids" takes you on an exciting trip into the world of AI. This book will show you the wonders of AI in a way that is both fun and easy to understand. The only requirement to read this book is that you are curious to learn about new things, and love the wonders of science and technology!

In this book, you will discover how AI is changing almost every aspect of our lives, and how it will become an important part of our future. You will learn about the interesting history of AI, from the first ideas about it in ancient times to the amazing innovations that led to its birth in the 1950s. You will be amazed at how AI works by learning about things like data, machine learning, code, computer vision, and natural language processing. Don't worry about the technical terms, they will be explained to you in ways that you can easily understand and use.

Follow along as AI develops and becomes a part of our daily lives, changing education, jobs, creativity, and even healthcare in big ways.

The book also talks about how important it is to use AI in an ethical fashion (to do the right things), and what risks it might bring if it is misused. We all start need to think about how we can use AI in a responsible way. This book tells you about what to look for when it comes to new information and tools, and it provides useful resources for you to learn more about AI, solve puzzles using your new knowledge, and learn how to code. Join Dr. Leo Lexicon on this incredible adventure!

Dr. Leo Lexicon is an educator and author. He is the founder of Lexicon Labs, a publishing imprint that is focused on creating entertaining books for active minds.

Table of Contents

1

What is AI?

INTRODUCTION

Have you ever asked Alexa to play your favorite song or seen Siri answer a question on an iPhone? Or perhaps you've seen a Tesla drive itself down the road or a robot vacuum a room on its own. These are all some visible uses of a really cool concept known as artificial intelligence, or what we will simply call AI. And I can bet you have heard all about the recent excitement over AI through the most famous chatbot ever made, ChatGPT. Maybe some of you have even tried typing into one of the many free AI bots now available on the Internet.

AI is a branch of computer science that tries to make computers behave more like humans do. However, AI is not a regular computer program that simply repeats the same calculations over and over. It is a unique kind of program that can make decisions similar to humans. At this point, it is still not as advanced as the human brain, but, with advances in new technologies, it is likely that AI will be much smarter and more capable in the future.

In this book, we will explore what AI is from many different perspectives. We shall see what today's AI can do, how it actually works behind the scenes, how it can change our own attitudes toward work and play, and how it can become a useful helper and assistant in many different human activities. If you are interested in science, and like to know how things work, this book is for you!

Common Uses of AI

Let's start by talking about how we use AI today. How much AI is already a part of our lives might surprise you. Usually, it is working in the background, helping us to do many complex tasks that may sometimes be boring, repetitive, or require a lot of calculations. At other times, it may be doing things that are really clever and creative, either with or without a human in charge.

- **Self-driving cars:** In the world of AI, "autonomous vehicles" refer to a vehicle's ability to navigate and move without human intervention. A great example of this is a self-driving car. Imagine yourself in a car, telling it where you want to go, perhaps to your friend's house or the park. The computer brain of the vehicle uses specialized sensors and cameras to view everything around it, including other vehicles, traffic signals, and even pedestrians crossing the street. It calculates the best route to your destination, and soon you are on your way. It has excellent driving skills, and it knows when to stop, turn, and move. Although self-driving cars are still in the early stages of development, they may one day make long drives much safer and more enjoyable! These are cars that can drive themselves. They use AI to see the road, understand traffic signs, and make decisions like when to stop or go. They can also get the latest updates on weather, traffic conditions, and other emergencies since they are connected to the Internet. Can you imagine all the calculations going on inside this onboard computer's head? Over time, this technology will become much more capable and dependable. A number of companies are already planning entire fleets of cars and trucks that are completely self-driving! In a few years, we are likely to be cruising down the highway in chauffeur-driven vehicles. And the chauffeur will be your car's self-driving AI!

- **Medical Diagnosis:** Next, consider a friend of yours who isn't feeling well and is exhibiting some strange symptoms. They go to the doctor for help, but it is not always easy for the doctor to pinpoint the exact problem. Further, the doctor may not be the right specialist for this particular situation, or simply be busy with a lot of other patients. This is where AI comes in. AI can function as the doctor's super-smart assistant. Today, we have medical AI applications that can examine a wide variety of images, including X-rays and scans, as well as a wealth of data regarding various illnesses. By doing this, AI can quickly discover patterns or hints that could assist the doctor in determining the cause of your friend's illness. Once the doctor provides a list of your friend's symptoms, and other measurements (like temperature, blood pressure, etc.), the AI gets to work on the problem. It is similar to having a very smart detective who can put all the pieces of the puzzle together and provide crucial information to the doctor to help them make the proper diagnosis. This aids the doctor in determining the best course of action for your friend's recovery. Besides helping doctors diagnose your condition, AI can also help discover new treatments, and provide patients with health-related advice. AI can therefore act as a helpful partner for doctors to solve medical mysteries and restore patients' health!

- **Customer Service:** Have you ever observed your parents purchasing a gift on the internet? Sometimes, they might need assistance selecting the ideal gift. Maybe they have too many options to choose from, or maybe they just can't find the right gift for the occasion. They might find themselves chatting with a special assistant known as a customer service bot rather than a live person. This bot is a helpful computer program that can understand your parents' questions and provide them with the appropriate responses. "What size shoes should I buy?" or "Where can I find a toy dinosaur?" are some examples of questions they might ask. The AI-powered bot can help determine what your parents need and provide it. It's like having an intelligent robot friend who is an expert shopper! The bot already has information about all the items in the store, and also knows how other shoppers go through the selection process. So, the next time you see your parents online chatting with a bot, whether for shopping or booking an airplane ticket, just know that AI is assisting them in obtaining the information they require.:

These simple examples demonstrate how AI is transforming the world around us. And guess what? It has only just begun. AI is going to change our world in a variety of fascinating ways, as long as we keep learning and inventing. Isn't it interesting to consider all the things AI is capable of? I hope you are settling in and are ready to explore AI's inner workings. We will get into this in more detail in the following chapter.

2

The Types of AI

DEFINING AI

Let us start the chapter by agreeing on how to define AI. We already talked about some examples that show you how AI actually works. In general, when computers are programmed to be extremely intelligent and perform tasks that typically require human intelligence, such as learning, problem-solving, and decision-making, this is known as artificial intelligence, or AI. This is the working definition of AI we will use for the rest of the book.

Typically, we can think of three types of AI: narrow AI, general AI, and super AI. Let us take a look at what we mean by these:

Narrow AI

Narrow AI is comparable to a computer that does well at only one specific task. It is similar to being an expert in a particular task, like understanding Egyptian hieroglyphs, or knowing all about planes, for example. Now consider a computer that is particularly good at playing the game of chess. It is a master chess player who is familiar with all the moves and tactics, and has learned how to play by analyzing thousands, if not millions, of games. However, because it is so focused on chess, if you asked it to do something else, like ride a bicycle or paint a picture, it wouldn't know how to do those things.

Another well-known example is a computer that can scan images and tell you whether a cat is present. This has actually been tried out at top technology companies as a test to see if the AI actually works. This computer can quickly respond, "Yes, there's a cat!" or "No, there isn't!" when you show it a picture because it has been trained to recognize what a cat looks like. However, due to its focus on finding cats, if you asked it to do something else, like tell you if an elephant was present in the image or count the number of trees in another image, it would be unable to do so.

General AI

The next type of AI we will look at is General AI. Now, General AI is similar to having a computer that is extremely intelligent, just like a very smart person. It has a wide range of abilities (as opposed to narrow ones), just like humans do. It can pick up new information, comprehend what it sees, and even perform tasks that we haven't explicitly taught it how to do. So, as you can see, it is quite different from narrow AI.

Think of a friend you have who is very intelligent and versatile. They are capable of telling jokes, playing sports, doing math, and painting stunning works of art. Everything they put their mind to, it seems like they pick up that skill very fast. That is how general AI operates. It can learn from humans and comprehend the knowledge we possess, enabling it to assist us with a variety of tasks.

Say you teach the general AI how to play the game of chess. Like the narrow AI whom we met earlier and who was an expert at playing chess, the general AI will pick up the game and get really good at it. The interesting part is that the general AI can also pick up other games like checkers or tic-tac-toe without having been explicitly taught those games. It can learn how to play new games by applying the knowledge it already possesses and using its powers of observation and analysis.

General AI is also capable of human-like comprehension. It can be taught to recognize various objects, animals, and even the definitions of words and sentences. It can therefore perform many tasks just like us and is comparable to a really smart computer friend. Even though we haven't taught it yet, it is capable of learning, comprehending, and performing new tasks. It's like having a super-smart assistant who can help us with a variety of tasks. You can now begin to see how general AI is a big leap from narrow AI. It can suddenly help us explore so many new areas and become a trusted assistant or co-pilot.

Super AI

Now, let's talk about the big kahuna: Super AI! Imagine being able to ask a computer any question and having the answer provided right away. Or if you could give it a particularly challenging mathematical equation to solve, it would quickly solve it. All of that and a whole lot more would be possible with super AI! No problem, however complex, is beyond its capacity to solve. It is like having a genius on speed dial.

Scientists are still working on developing super AI, but it might take some time given how difficult it is. They want to make sure it is secure and has practical applications. They want to be extremely cautious and ensure that there won't be any issues that cause things to go wrong. We will get to the reasons why we need to be very careful while developing a capability like Super AI in a later chapter.

University research labs, companies, and the government are all spending millions of dollars every year on this research. And who knows? Perhaps we will soon have computers that are much smarter than anyone could have ever imagined. It is a fascinating concept to consider!

Now that we know what AI is, and what the different types of AI can do, it is important to understand that it took many years of research and the work of many brilliant minds to get here. In the next chapter, we will look at the brief history of AI.

3

A Brief History of AI

Just like you have a story about your life, AI has its own story too! The history of AI is like an adventure filled with amazing ideas, big dreams, and even some surprises. And just like any other technology, it has had its share of ups and downs.

KEY MILESTONES IN AI HISTORY

Let's step into our time machine and explore some of the key milestones in the history of AI.

Imagining AI (Ancient Times to the 1940s)

Humans have been dreaming of great ideas since time immemorial. Even though they didn't have computers back then, even ancient people came up with stories and myths about machines with superpowers by using their imaginations. They told stories about amazing 'machines' that could talk, walk, and do amazing things; sometimes these machines were in the form of animals or even other humans with special skills and knowledge. Even though these stories didn't involve real AI, they showed something very important: people have always been interested in tools that can think. They wanted to make something that could think, learn, and solve problems in the same way that modern humans do. But these were just nice dreams until the 1940s, when we first started making computers! Unlike the computers we use today, these early ones were big and heavy, but they were a first step toward making AI a reality. Of course, it took many more decades before computers became smaller, faster, and cheaper. As soon as computers were invented, scientists and engineers started working hard to teach them how to think and learn. It was a hard trip, but they got farther as they went. And they had no idea that their work would lead to the amazing AI that is all around us and helps us in so many ways today.

The Birth of AI (1950s)

Our next stop is the 1950s. Alan Turing was a very smart man who was thinking about a very important question: "Can machines think like humans?". His breakthrough was that he was able to create a machine that could turn thought processes into numbers. This would be the first step in a long quest to try and answer the clever question he had posed. He wanted to know if a machine could be so smart that a person talking to it would actually think they were talking to a real person. This is the idea behind the famous 'Turing Test'. We will find out more about this test, but what is interesting is that we still don't have a computer that has passed this test! Many experts now think that we are only a few years away from this mission being accomplished.

Alan Turing, considered the father of modern computer science

Here is how the Turing Test works. You sit down in front of a computer and start talking to it like you would with a friend in a chat window. There's a catch, though! You're not sure if you're talking to a real person (at the other end) or a computer. The computer does its best to act like a person and answer your questions in a way that makes you think it's a real person. Now it's up to you to listen carefully to the answers and responses in the chat and try to figure out what's going on. If you think you might be talking to a computer, you can ask tricky questions or talk about things that only a real person would know. The computer has to work very hard to make you believe it's a person. The Turing Test says that a computer passes if it can make you think it's a person. But if you can tell it's a computer instead of a person, the computer still needs to learn more. The Turing Test is a simple concept, but it is a fun way to test how smart a computer is. It is a way for scientists and programmers to try and improve their artificial intelligence technology. Who knows, maybe one day you'll get to take part in a Turing Test and see how good computers have gotten at acting like people.

Another important event happened in 1956, when a chemist named John McCarthy did something very special. He went to a big conference at Dartmouth College and used a new word there. "Artificial Intelligence," or "AI" for short, was the word. It was like a special name for machines that could think and learn like people. AI was officially born at that meeting, so it is a very important event. So, Alan Turing and John McCarthy gave us the early ideas for machines that are very smart and can do amazing things. They can fix problems, learn new things, and even talk to us like we're friends. Isn't it cool that these smart people from the past helped make AI a real thing? It's like they set out on a big journey that has given us amazing technology and new ways to get things done.

The Roller-Coaster Years (1960s-1990s)

From the 1960s to the 1990s, after AI was invented, there were some ups and downs, like taking a roller coaster ride. People were sometimes really excited about AI and all the cool things it could do. But there were also times when they felt let down because making AI was a lot harder than they thought it would be. You see, it turned out to be hard to make computers think and learn like people. It wasn't as simple as turning on a switch to make it happen. Along the way, scientists and other smart people had to figure out a lot of hard things and solve hard problems.

But they didn't give up, even when things got hard. They kept working and learning, trying out new ideas, and coming up with ways to improve AI. Even though there were some bumps in the road, they knew that it was all part of the way to making something amazing. When you're working on a big project or trying to learn something new, you might run into problems and feel a little down. But like those experts, you should never give up and always keep going. Ups and downs are fine because they help us learn and grow. And the programmers and scientists who worked during this period were very determined to see their project succeed.

AI Gets Smart (Late 90s–2000s)

Now we zoom forward to the late 1990s. This is when AI started to get really smart! One of the most interesting things that happened was that AI started beating people at board games. How could that be? We are aware that chess grandmasters are typically among the smartest people alive, with extraordinary memories and minds that have undergone endless study and practice. But now, here were the computers, winning games like chess and making it seem very easy indeed. This was a big deal because it showed how far artificial intelligence had come. It showed people that computers could do things that were hard for even the smartest people to do. It was like a friendly battle between people and computers, and the computers were getting really good at it!

Fig. Kasparov is Stunned by Deep Blue (Source: The New York Times)

Deep Blue was an extremely intelligent supercomputer that the company **IBM** had trained to play chess. A challenge match was set up between Deep Blue and the then-reigning World Chess Champion, Garry Kasparov. They had a big contest, and what do you think happened? On May 11th, 1997, Deep Blue won the match. A momentous day in AI history! The story made headlines all over the world, and people began to see how smart computers had become. Deep Blue had proven that computers could learn to play complicated games like chess and become the best at them. Deep Blue was in fact so powerful that it could calculate 100 million to 200 million chess moves per second! It was an exciting time for AI and an important milestone that we still remember. Deep Blue's victory showed that AI could not only calculate and memorize but also strategize and make decisions, just like a human. And it made people wonder: if an AI can play chess this well, what else could it do in the future? And we didn't have to wait long. The research efforts in AI took off, and steady progress was made over the next couple of decades.

In the year 2011, something extraordinary happened on a popular TV game show called Jeopardy! The show was all about answering trivia questions, and contestants had to be really smart to win. But guess what? A special computer named Watson joined the competition! IBM was back in the news; this time, they had developed Watson, a super-smart computer. It had been trained with lots and lots of information, like books, encyclopedias, and even information on the internet. Watson could understand and process all that information really fast, much faster than any human could. So, when Watson competed on Jeopardy!, it was like a big test for artificial intelligence. Could a computer beat the best human players at their own game? And you know what? Watson did it! It competed against two amazing human champions and won first place!

Again, this was a really big deal in the evolution of AI because it showed us just how far computers could go in understanding and answering questions like humans. It proved that AI had the power to learn, think, and compete in the world of knowledge.

Watson's win opened up new possibilities for AI in areas like education, medicine, and many more. Isn't it crazy to think about how computers got to be so smart and powerful? Who knows what else AI will be able to do in the future that will be really cool? It's so exciting to think about all the things that could happen!

AI In Everyday Life (2010s - Today)

The story of the evolution of AI took another important step in 2016. And, believe it or not, it was also centered around a board game!

Imagine playing a game of checkers with your friend. You have to think about where to move your pieces to "jump" over your friend's pieces, right? Now, imagine a game that's even more challenging than checkers, with a bigger board and more pieces. That game is called Go, and it's one of the hardest games in the world! Go is an ancient board game that originated in China over 2,500 years ago. It's played on a big square board with lots of lines (19 lines by 19 lines, to be exact!). Two players take turns placing black and white stones on the board, trying to surround more territory than their opponent. What makes Go so complicated is the number of possible moves at any given time. In fact, there are more possible positions in Go than there are atoms in the universe!

Now, let's bring AI into the picture. In 2016, something amazing happened. An AI named AlphaGo, created by a company called DeepMind, played Go against one of the best human players in the world—and won! This was a big surprise because, remember, Go is super complicated. For AlphaGo to win, it had to be really good at learning, making smart decisions, and analyzing millions of possible combinations.

The reason why AI beating a human at Go is considered another key milestone is because it showed just how far AI had come in a short span of time. It wasn't just following a set of instructions; it was thinking and strategizing, similar to how a human would play. And remember, the game of Go is so complicated that no human could possibly memorize all the possible moves. So, AlphaGo wasn't just remembering moves; it was really understanding the game.

This was a sign that AI had taken a big step forward. It gave scientists hope that one day AI might be able to help solve other complex problems, like curing diseases or predicting weather changes, since these problems are extremely complex and hard to solve. And all of this from learning to play a game! Isn't that incredible?

Our final stop is today. AI is all around us now! It helps us find information online; it recommends songs and movies we might like; and it even powers self-driving cars. And this is just the beginning. Scientists and engineers are always coming up with new ways to improve AI technology. Today, AI has gotten so good that it can even make art and stories on its own. There are AI models like ChatGPT ("Chat Generative Pre-trained Transformer") and BARD (which stands for "Behaviorally Augmented Robot Design") that can talk to people and even write poems, stories, and songs. It's like having a partner who can help us think of new ideas and work together.

We can safely conclude that AI is here to stay. In the years ahead, it is going to transform our lives in infinite ways.

4

How AI Works

Welcome to the exciting world of how AI works! To make it fun, let us imagine that AI is in training to be a superhero. In order to get there, it has to learn how to develop and use its superpowers. There are several things that need to happen first before the AI can truly shine in terms of demonstrating what it is capable of. In order to better understand this process, let's talk about data, machine learning, and programming.

Data

AI data is like the instruction manual for a superhero. It's like a giant book or 'database' that contains all the information our superhero needs to use their superpowers efficiently. AI requires data to comprehend and learn about the world, just as our superhero needs knowledge of his or her abilities and how to use them. Imagine that our superhero wants to fly a plane. They must know all about aircraft mechanics, how the wind affects flight, how much force to apply during takeoff, and safe landing techniques. All of this information functions as our superhero's data. They study and train in it to get better at flying. Similar to the example we discussed earlier about getting an AI to identify cats in a picture, it takes a lot of data before the AI starts to comprehend what a cat actually looks like. It can start by truly understanding the unique characteristics of cats, such as their pointed ears, furry bodies, and tails.

Pictures are, of course, one type of data. Data itself can take many different forms. Images, text, sounds, or even numbers are all acceptable. For instance, we can provide AI with a large database of song lyrics as data if we want it to write a catchy tune. The AI can learn how to write melodies and lyrics that go well together by examining the patterns in the lyrics.

As we can already see, data is like a gold mine of knowledge that AI can discover, learn from, absorb, and reinterpret to create something new and unique. Similar to how our superhero must read their manual to learn how to use their powers, AI uses data to train and enhance its skills. AI can learn more and become more adept the more varied and plentiful the data is.

Machine Learning

Now let's imagine that our superhero trainee is working on a new skill called machine learning. The goal this time is for them to master a musical instrument like the guitar. When our friend first picks up the guitar, they might find it difficult to produce any enjoyable tones. They might strum in the wrong direction or press the wrong strings. They're only beginning to learn, so it's okay. They gain knowledge from their mistakes and get a little bit better each time they practice playing the guitar. They might discover that gently strumming the strings produces a soft sound or that pressing particular strings in specific locations produces different notes. They become more proficient and begin to play melodies that sound more and more like music with each practice session. That and machine learning are very similar! It's about growing over time and learning from mistakes. A computer or robot can learn to play the guitar by practicing and making adjustments based on what works and what doesn't, just like our superhero friend.

Similar to how our superhero friend uses practice and feedback, the computer or robot uses a lot of information when learning new skills. It learns how to make lovely melodies and rhythms by examining the musical patterns. It learns how to strum the strings to produce various sounds as well as which notes to play in what order.

Machine learning is comparable to our superhero friend learning to play the guitar, in that regard. It's about getting better through experience, practice, and making mistakes. Through machine learning, a computer or robot can improve at tasks, judgment calls, or problem-solving just as our superhero friend improves at playing the guitar with practice. They can learn and develop thanks to this incredible superpower!

Programming

If Machine Learning is the superhero's power and data is the instruction manual, then programming is the superhero's training coach. Programming is the way we tell our AI superheroes what to do and how to learn.

This time, let us assume that our superhero pal has the ability to become a fantastic cook. But they require direction on what recipes to follow, what ingredients to use, and how to prepare delectable meals if they are to become culinary masters. Programming comes into play here!

Programming is similar to designing a unique workout plan for our superhero chef. They are given instructions on what to do and how to learn, much like a step-by-step manual. Programming gives the superhero the instructions and methods to become a great cook, just like a coach in the kitchen. We can create a program that instructs our super-chef how to prepare recipes, gather ingredients, mix ingredients, and cook foods in the proper order. It's comparable to the chef's private coach saying, "Start by combining the flour, sugar, and eggs to make a delicious cake. Then bake it in the oven for a specific amount of time and at a specific temperature."

This way, our superhero chef can learn new cooking techniques and accurately follow recipes thanks to programming. They can be programmed to sample various cuisines, discover flavors, and try out unusual pairings. Programming gives our superheroes the instructions to improve their culinary skills, just like a coach helps a chef try out new techniques.

Programming also enables us to assign objectives and difficulties to our superhero chef. We can program them to prepare a three-course meal in a certain amount of time or to prepare a particular dish using a particular recipe. A chef's coach might set up challenges to help them hone their skills and express their creativity in the kitchen.

Our super chef can learn, adapt, and produce delicious meals through programming. It's like giving them a personalized training program that makes it possible for them to transform into culinary superstars!

Thus, programming is essential when using AI. We are actively creating a training program for our AI, complete with guidelines, tricks, and challenges to improve their abilities, whether it is in cooking or a host of other useful skills.

So, as we can see from the breakdown above, our AI superhero starts off not knowing much and is essentially a novice student. But with lots of data (the instruction manual) and good programming (the training coach), they learn and improve using Machine Learning (their superpower). AI might seem complicated, but when you break it down, it's like a superhero learning to save the day. And the most exciting part? We're the ones who get to teach them and see where their superpowers take us next!

Other Superpowers

We already talked about machine learning as AI's first superpower. Let us look at two other common superpowers that today's AI models are already capable of.

Computer Vision

For computers and robots, computer vision is a superpower that literally helps them see. Computer vision enables machines and robots to see and comprehend the world in a similar way to how you use your eyes to see the world around you. It enables them to see images or videos and identify what they contain, much like how you can see an image and immediately recognize that it is a cat or a car. It's like giving them the ability to use sophisticated algorithms and specialized technology to comprehend and make sense of the things they "see." By analyzing and comprehending what it sees, just like your eyes and brain do, computer vision enables robots and computers to navigate, identify objects, and even play games!

For a better understanding of computer vision, let's look at another example. Let's create a game we call "Guess the Animal." You have to identify the animal from the hints I give you about it. You use your eyes to study the animal's image and take note of its features. A little bit like that, but for AI, is computer vision!

In the field of computer vision, artificial intelligence (AI) can examine images or videos and recognize what's there. It is capable of identifying things, animals, and even people. When viewing images or videos, it can exclaim, "Hey, that's a cat!" It understands that the cat is a living creature and can recognize the various features of the cat, such as its eyes, nose, and tail. Numerous innovative uses exist for computer vision. Have you heard of phone face filters? Computer vision is used when you apply a filter to your face that gives you silly ears and whiskers. The filter's AI recognizes your face and places the humorous elements where they belong.

Security systems also employ computer vision. Have you ever seen surveillance cameras in places like banks or airports? If someone is attempting to do something that they shouldn't be doing, they can use computer vision to detect it. The AI can identify unusual activity or objects and notify security personnel.

Why is computer vision so important? Well, imagine if you had to navigate your world without being able to see anything. It would be pretty hard, wouldn't it? For a long time, that's what it was like for computers. But with computer vision, we're giving them a sort of 'sight' to better understand the world around them. Who knows what other exciting things AI and computer vision will be able to do in the future? Maybe they'll help explore space or deep under the ocean, or maybe even help with your homework! Isn't it amazing to think about all the things AI can do with the power of 'sight'? Next time you use your phone or play a video game, remember that there's a superhero power at work right there in your hands!

Natural Language Processing (NLP)

Next, let's consider a superpower called natural language processing. Let's say you are speaking with a friend. Due to your understanding of word meanings and how sentences are put together, your grammar, and your vocabulary, you can comprehend what they are saying. NLP, then, is sort of like an exclusive ability that AI has to comprehend and interpret language like we do! It is a clever technique through which

AI can comprehend language in the same way that humans do.

NLP enables Siri or other voice assistants to comprehend your questions and give you responses when you speak to them. What's the weather like today, let's say? NLP examines the words in your query to assist the AI in understanding that you are inquiring about the weather. It then retrieves the pertinent data and informs you whether it is sunny, rainy, or snowy outside. When you type on a computer or smartphone, NLP is also at work. Have you ever noticed that your device will occasionally fill in the rest of a word for you as you start typing it? That is also NLP in action! It appears as though your computer is reading what you are typing and attempting to guess which word you will use next based on what you have already typed. You can save time, and it's very convenient!

We can begin to see that NLP functions by breaking up sentences and then trying to comprehend the significance of each word. In order to understand the overall message, it searches for patterns and connections among the words. It is capable of handling even complex issues like idioms, slang, and different languages. NLP enables AI to comprehend the relationships between various speech components, such as nouns, verbs, and adjectives. Try asking ChatGPT a question in slang, and there is a good chance it will understand it perfectly.

AI is able to comprehend a sentence's context thanks to NLP. For instance, if you say, "I saw a bat," NLP can determine, based on the words around you or the topic of conversation, whether you are referring to the animal or a baseball bat. It's comparable to having a language detective who deciphers hints to determine what you mean. Or, if you are talking about sports bats, it can determine if you are talking about baseball, softball, cricket, or stickball! It all boils down to the overall context of the conversation you are having.

NLP is a unique and important tool that AI employs to comprehend and respond to us in a language that we regularly use. AI acquires language through NLP in a similar way to how we do as we develop, making it an intelligent and useful part of our daily lives. What could be more human than that?

5

How AI will Remake Education

Let's go on a trip to a place you go almost every day: your classroom! But hold on; this isn't just any classroom. It is a futuristic school where AI plays a central role in helping you learn. Now, doesn't that sound exciting? Let's explore some possibilities.

AI As a Learning Buddy

Imagine having a special friend who knows exactly what you like, what you find easy, and what makes you really happy. This friend is like your personal teacher, who can help you learn by giving you the right tasks or books. What is different is that it can do this for every single student by focusing on their own individual strengths and weaknesses. This is one of the ways AI can help you along your learning path. The term for this is "personalized learning."

This teacher goes the extra mile. AI can make sure that you learn at the right pace. AI can help you get better at something hard by giving you more chances to do it or making sure you revise the material well before attempting new challenges. When you get good at something, AI can give you harder tasks to keep you learning. AI helps make sure that your learning is neither too easy nor too hard, but just right. This is cool because it can tell you if you are doing something right or if you need to try again. This helps you learn more quickly and feel better about how well you're doing.

Not only can it help you improve how well you learn, but it can also help you figure out what kinds of things you like to learn about. If you're really interested in a subject, AI can suggest more things to look into and ask you questions that will make you think. It's like having a friend who always knows what to show you based on your interests and abilities.

Now you may think that interacting with a computer all day is not going to be much fun. But AI can also help you work with other kids who like the same things you do. It can connect you with people who are far away so you can learn together, talk about your ideas, and work on projects as a team. It's like having a virtual school where you can meet people and learn together.

But keep in mind that AI won't replace your teachers. Its purpose is to help them. Your teachers are still important because they can understand how you feel, cheer you up when you're sad, and help you in ways that AI can't. AI is just a tool that helps you learn in a way that is more fun and fits your needs. But there is no doubt that AI will be used more and more, both in the classroom at school and at your study desk at home.

So, if you have AI as your special learning partner, you can have a great time learning things that are just right for you. It lets you learn at your own pace, gives you fun tasks, and makes sure you have fun while learning. Get ready for a great time learning new things with the help of your AI learning buddy.

AI As the Teacher's Super Assistant

Just like it can help you, AI can also help your teachers in ways that are like having a great assistant. That's right! AI is here to help teachers teach and help kids like you learn and grow even better. Imagine if your teacher had a special ability that let her know right away what each student needed. They could tell who needs help with spelling, who is ready for harder math questions, and who just did a great job in science. Well, AI gives teachers this awesome ability to look at each student's progress and see exactly what they need.

AI can gather and examine data about how each student is doing, what their strengths are, and where they might need more help. This means that teachers can spend more time doing what they love and are best at: teaching, leading, and inspiring you! AI can help teachers make lessons just for you that are tailored to your needs. It can suggest tasks, games, or even videos based on what you like and how you learn best. So, if you are interested in dinosaurs, AI can suggest books or websites that you can use to learn more about them. If you like to solve puzzles, AI can give you suggestions for fun math games that will test your mind. With the help of AI, teachers can make learning more fun and fit it to your needs.

AI can also help your teacher plan lessons in a more effective way. It can give them ideas, help them find tools, and even help them plan their days. So, your teacher will have more time to plan great lessons and be fully present to help you learn and answer your questions.

But remember that your teacher is still the most important person in the classroom, even with all the cool things AI can do. They are there to understand your feelings, help you when you need it, and make sure everyone feels safe and cared for. AI is just there to help your teacher, like a reliable helper. The next time you see your teacher using AI in the classroom, know that it's there to make their job even better. It helps them understand you better and make lessons that are just right for you. Your teacher can shine even brighter and help you become the best learner you can be if they have AI as their super-assistant.

The AI-Powered Classroom of the Future

This is one area that's going to truly revolutionize your lives. As the capabilities of AI grow, your classroom and how you learn could be completely transformed by AI. We are still in the early days of AI use in education, but there is no doubt that big changes are coming. You'd have more chances to learn in the way that suits you best. You could explore the subjects you love in new and exciting ways. And your teacher would be able to support you even better than they can now.

But remember, AI in education, like a pencil or a book, is a tool. The real magic happens when you use it to learn, grow, and create. Just imagine what you could do with AI as your learning buddy. In the future, your classroom might look very different. But one thing won't change: the joy of learning. So, get ready to step into this amazing future. With AI by your side, who knows what you'll discover next? Your educational adventure is just beginning!

6

How AI Will Change Jobs and Creativity

Do you remember how we talked about the superpowers of AI, like seeing like people and talking like us? AI doesn't just hang out and do cool things with its skills. It is actually put to use, helping out in hospitals, on highways, and even in your best video games. Let's go on a quick trip to see where AI is being used.

AI CHANGES JOBS

AI, The Super Doctor and Nurse

We go to the hospital when we don't feel well, right? But did you know that AI is also used? in hospitals to help doctors and nurses? AI can look at X-rays and photos to find anything strange. Think of AI as a super nurse with x-ray vision who can see things that humans might not be able to. AI makes it faster for people to get the right medicine.

AI, The Incredible Driver

Have you ever wished that cars could drive themselves? Well, thanks to AI, that's no longer just a dream! Self-driving cars are like having your own driver. AI helps them see the road, read traffic signs, and know when to stop and when to go. They can take you safely to school, the park, or a sports game without a person behind the wheel. It's like riding on a magic cloud with wheels.

AI, The Magician Who Makes People Happy

Let's now go somewhere fun: the world of entertainment. Have you ever played a video game against a robot player who was really good? That's what AI is! It remembers what you do, makes the game harder, and keeps you busy for hours. And when you watch your favorite shows or movies on streaming services like Disney or Netflix, AI is working in the background. It's like a movie magician, guessing what shows you might like based on what you've already watched. So, remember to thank AI the next time you find a cool new show.

But guess what, AI doesn't stop where people usually do. It also takes on some jobs that are very unusual. AI tells farmers when and how much to water and feed their crops to keep them healthy. It even helps scientists find patterns and other things in the stars that would take people a long time to find. In the world of fashion, AI can tell you what clothes you might like, almost like a personal planner. And when it comes to art, AI can make new, unique pieces. It's like having a very sophisticated friend who can help you in any field!

AI is hard at work in every part of our world, making things faster, safe, and a lot more fun. There are so many options! What do you think might happen next with AI? Can you think of other cool jobs that AI might do in the future? Remember that AI is probably with you every time you play a game, watch a movie, or even ride in a car.

CAN AI BE CREATIVE?

Now you may be wondering if AI can really be creative and clever like Picasso or Einstein. Can it think of crazy and unusual ideas or get inspired like smart humans do? That's a great question! Let's get right into it.

AI is more creative in different ways than people usually are. AI doesn't get ideas from things like seeing a beautiful sky or feeling happy. It doesn't have sudden "light bulb" moments like we do. Instead, AI uses the trends and information it has learned to make something new. Do you remember that amazing cookbook we were talking about? Well, that's kind of how AI works. It has looked at a lot of drawings and songs and learned the different "recipes" or ways that they were made. Then, it takes those ideas and combines them in new and interesting ways to make its own art or music.

So, even though AI doesn't have feelings or experiences like we do, it can still make amazing things that surprise and please us. It can use what it has learned from looking at a lot of paintings or songs to make something new and interesting. AI can sometimes come up with ideas that humans may not have thought of. Its ability to look for trends and make sense of information can lead to surprising and creative outcomes. It's like having a friend who sees the world differently and looks at art and music from a different angle.

So, AI's imagination might not be the same as ours, but it can still make amazing and new things that catch our attention. It can make art and music that make us think, feel, and see the beauty of creativity in new ways. Isn't it interesting?

Remember that there are many ways to be creative, and AI is just one of them. It gives art and music a whole new depth and shows us that there are a lot of ways to be creative. So, let's enjoy the unique creativity of AI and keep getting ideas from the surprising and fun things it makes!

The Creative Duo is You and AI

Imagine a world where you work together with AI to make great art and music, design a home, or create a new videogame. People can be creative on their own, but they can also work with AI to come up with new ideas and styles. This is a very exciting idea, and it's already happening! This is where the real potential of AI lies—in being your partner in a new creative journey.

For example, AI can be a creative partner for artists and help them come up with new ideas. They can put their own artwork into the AI and ask it to make changes or suggest new styles. Artists can try out ideas they might not have thought of on their own when they work together. It's like having an artist's helper who brings a whole new set of brushes and colors to the table.

AI can also help artists make interesting sounds and rhythms. AI can look at a lot of music and come up with new tunes or chord progressions based on what it has learned. Musicians can work with AI to try out different pairings and arrangements. This can lead to compositions that go beyond what is usually considered "music." It's like having a musical friend who makes your songs more interesting and surprising.

Image inspired by A Medieval Painting (created by Midjourney AI)

The way people and AI work together is a true creative relationship. When we work together, we can make something even more amazing than what any of us could do on our own. When you and your friends come up with great ideas by bouncing them off each other, it's like teamwork at school. AI gives us a new point of view and new ways to explore, which lets us push the limits of our imagination.

Imagine that the next time you draw, sing, or dance, you can think about what it would be like to work with AI. You could paint with pixels and use AI's methods along with your artistic skills to make beautiful digital art. Or maybe you'll write songs with the help of AI, combining your sense of music with its ability to compute to make mesmerizing tunes.

7

Dangers of AI and The Need for Ethical AI

WHAT IS ETHICAL BEHAVIOR?

Being ethical entails acting morally (doing the right thing) and treating others fairly (not discriminating). It means showing people respect, kindness, and honesty. When we make decisions, we must consider what is right and just, and we strive to make choices that will benefit others and improve the world.

Think about a toy you have that your friend would really like to play with. Sharing the toy with your friend as opposed to keeping it all to yourself would be ethical. Fairness and taking into account how your actions may affect others are key. Being ethical also means being honest and telling the truth. It means that you accept responsibility for any damage you unintentionally cause, even if it means getting into trouble. It is about upholding morality even when it is not the most convenient course of action.

Being ethical also means that we treat everyone equally and refrain from discriminating against anyone based on their appearance, origin, or any other factor. It's about including everyone and showing respect for everyone, regardless of who they are.

Making decisions that are fair, kind, and honest is therefore the essence of ethics. It involves acting morally and taking into account how our decisions affect other people. We can all live in a better world if we make an effort to be moral beings.

THE IMPORTANCE OF ETHICS IN AI

We just saw what being ethical means for us humans. Now imagine a robot, computer, or AI system having to make those same decisions. For them, it's even trickier! This is where the concept of "AI ethics" becomes important.

We refer to computers or robots as having artificial intelligence (AI) when they behave intelligently and make decisions that resemble those of humans. But there are several problems that come up once we hand over these decisions to an AI.

Firstly, these AIs are not able to judge right from wrong or make difficult choices based on what's fair or kind because they don't have feelings like we do. Can we design a system so that it thinks more like a human?

Another problem is that AI can occasionally be biased. That means that it might come to unfairly biased conclusions. For instance, if an AI system is trained using unfair information, it might end up treating individuals unfairly based on their gender or skin tone. How do we train an AI to be fair and not discriminate?

AI can also look at a lot of personal information about people from various sources, such as where they live or what they enjoy. But many may consider this intrusive and would not like their private data to be used in this way. While using AI to aid us, we must be careful to protect people's privacy. Can we ensure privacy while building better AI?

Who is accountable when something goes wrong is another issue. Who should be held liable if an AI system harms someone or makes a poor decision? Answering that question is difficult. If we do not think about this carefully while we design the system, somebody could get hurt or even killed! For example, AI is occasionally used in products like military robots and self-driving cars. Should these types of AI always put others at risk in order to protect the person using them? These are difficult decisions that require careful consideration.

Soldier of the Future? AI-powered Humanoid Robot

People who work in ethics and AI are attempting to establish rules and regulations to address these issues. They want to ensure that AI is fair, respects individuals' privacy, and adheres to what we believe to be right and good. In order to ensure that everyone's voice is heard, they also want to involve a variety of people and solicit their opinions.

Therefore, to put it simply, teaching computers and robots to make moral decisions, to be fair, and to respect others' privacy is what is meant by ethics in AI. In a similar way to how we have our own rules for being good and acting morally, it's like giving them a set of guidelines to follow. In this manner, AI can benefit us and improve the world. It is very important that we sort out the right approaches to these questions because AI is going to be with us for a long time. We want to make sure that it acts responsibly and makes decisions that are similar to what humans would make. In fact, there is a technical term for this in AI; we call it 'alignment'. AI systems should be 'aligned' to the same values that humans commonly use to conduct their affairs.

DEVELOPING FUTURE AI

We can help make sure that AI is used to create a future that is just, safe, and beneficial for all people if we ask these important questions about ethics and artificial intelligence (AI). Therefore, the next time you interact with AI or observe it in action, keep these big questions in mind and think about them. Because you won't just be using AI in the future; you'll also be inventing it, programming it, and making decisions about how to use it. You will determine how AI develops in the years to come. In the next chapter, we will look at how you can get involved!

8

Get Involved!

You might be wondering why it's so important for young people like you to get involved in artificial intelligence at this point. There are many reasons. Learning about AI can be a lot of fun! It is like discovering a whole new world, one in which machines can learn and think for themselves. If you get involved in artificial intelligence (AI), you will have the opportunity to help shape the future and find out how this technology can make our lives better. And, believe it or not, many of you already have the skills and experience to start learning about AI. If you are familiar with Lego, Mindstorms, or Scratch, consider yourself hired!

Next, you can improve your ability to solve problems and think critically by starting early with artificial intelligence (AI) education. You will learn new ways to be creative as well as explore the inner workings of various technical systems. Learning about AI will make you a more knowledgeable user who is able to make well-informed decisions and use technology in a responsible manner. Prepare to enter the exciting world of AI and have a good time while you learn about all the incredible things it is capable of doing.

KEY AREAS TO LOOK INTO

Artificial intelligence (AI) is a really interesting field for young people to get involved in since it will put you on a journey to understand how computers function and how they can come to intelligent conclusions. You can educate yourself on algorithms, which are comparable to detailed instructions that tell computers what actions to carry out. There is also the possibility of looking into machine learning, which is when computers can learn from data and improve their decision-making skills over time.

There is more to artificial intelligence than what we see in movies or read about in books. It permeates every aspect of our day-to-day existence. We have already covered many examples where creative thinking, programming skills, and the ability to analyze information and design new systems become very important. We know how voice assistants, smart robots, self-driving cars, and video games can all incorporate AI. It is very exciting to see how AI is going to make our lives simpler and more enjoyable in the future.

Finally, when we study artificial intelligence, we also study the ethics of the field. Being just and equal consideration to everyone are essential components of ethical behavior. It is critical to ensure that artificial intelligence does not engage in unethical behavior or invade the privacy of individuals. We have a duty to employ AI in a manner that is both beneficial and positive. We can ensure that AI is used in a manner that is fair and respectful if we have an understanding of the ethical considerations that are involved with it. It all boils down to making the world a better place for people of all walks of life!

It is a fantastic opportunity for us to use technology in a way that demonstrates our curiosity, creativity, and responsibility. It is the beginning of an adventurous voyage, and the ship is about to sail off from the harbor! In the next few sections, I will provide you with a lot of links to resources and tools that will help you on your journey.

WEBSITES TO VISIT

These websites are wonderful resources that will help you on your journey toward becoming more knowledgeable about AI. They will instill in you an appreciation for important concepts, encourage you to participate in hands-on activities, and pique your curiosity about the incredible potential of AI. Therefore, get ready to embark on an amazing journey into the world of artificial intelligence by exploring the websites listed here.

1. **Artificial Intelligence Research at Code.org (https://code.org/ai):**

    The AI Exploration on Code.org is analogous to a treasure map that leads you into the world of artificial intelligence through the use of coding! It teaches you how to create your own artificial intelligence programs by providing tutorials and projects that are broken down into step-by-step instructions. You will learn how machines can learn and make decisions just like humans can if you follow these coding activities and do them in the correct order.

2. **Machine Learning for Kids (https://machinelearningforkids.co.uk/):**

   Teaching a computer to recognize images or sounds in the same way that you do is an example of machine learning, which is explained in more detail below. You are able to accomplish exactly that with Machine Learning for Kids. You can even teach the computer something new using the webcam you have on your computer. It's just like having fun with your computer by playing a game!

3. **Experiments with Google (https://experiments.withgoogle.com/):**

   Google wants to know if you're the type of person who enjoys trying new things. Experiments with Google are comparable to a large playground in which one can participate in a wide variety of games and activities. Similar to how it works in a game, you can train a computer to recognize your drawings or the sounds you make. It's a ton of exciting fun!

4. **Cognimates (http://cognimates.me/home/):** Have you ever considered creating your own video games or writing code for robots? You can do all of that and more with Cognimates at your disposal! You also have the option of training your own AI models, which is analogous to instructing a computer to think in the same way that you do. Watching this awesome video will educate you further on the subject.

5. **AI 4 Children (https://www.ai4children.org/):** AI 4 Children is a place where you can learn about Artificial Intelligence, which is a

fancy way of saying "teaching computers to think like humans." AI 4 Children is a place where you can learn about Artificial Intelligence. You will be using a language known as Scratch, which is an enjoyable and straightforward method for getting started with learning about AI.

LEARNING TO CODE

These tools and resources for coding are like superpowers that will help you learn about AI. They make coding fun, creative, and easy to learn. They also let you bring your ideas to life and learn about AI in a hands-on way. So, get ready to code, build, and find out what amazing things you can do with these amazing tools and resources.

1. **Scratch (https://scratch.mit.edu/):** Scratch is a fun and easy-to-use website where you can make your own interactive stories, games, and animations to learn how to code. To make cool things happen on the computer screen, it's like playing with building blocks. You can let your mind run wild and make your ideas come to life with Scratch.

2. **Cozmo Robot (https://www.anki.com/en-us/cozmo):** Cozmo is a cute and smart robot friend who can help you learn and have fun. You can talk to Cozmo on your phone or tablet, teach it new tricks, and even use coding blocks to make it do cool things. It's like having a robot friend to help you learn about AI.

3. **LEGO Mindstorms (https://www.lego.com/en-us/themes/mindstorms:**

   With LEGO Mindstorms, you can build and program your own robots in a great way. With LEGO bricks, motors, and sensors, you can make robots that can move, see what's around them, and do what you tell them to do. If you learn how to code them, you can bring them to life and have a lot of fun with them.

4. **Python:** AI developers often use Python, which is a popular programming language. It's like learning a secret code that only computers can understand. You can look into Python if you want to learn more about AI. Codecademy has a Python course just for kids. In this course, you can learn Python step by step and improve your coding skills.

5. **Python.org (http://www.python.org/):** Python's official site is at Python.org. It has a lot of helpful Python tools and information. If you want to learn how to code on your own computer, you can look at tutorials, examples, and even download Python software.

6. **Codecademy's Python Course (https://www.codecademy.com/learn/learn-python):**

   The Python course for kids on Codecademy is a fun and hands-on way for kids to learn Python. It walks you through lessons and exercises that teach you the basics of Python coding. You'll write code and see the results right away, which is very cool.

So, dear AI explorers, it is time to go on an amazing journey with these great tools and resources! With Scratch, Cozmo Robot, and LEGO Mindstorms, you can show off your creativity, problem-solving skills, and imagination. With each click, block, or robot you make, you'll learn more about AI and the amazing things you can do with code and robots. Don't forget to check out resources like Codecademy and Python.org that can help you learn how to code. They are the secret keys you need to unlock AI's full potential. By looking into these resources, you'll learn useful information and skills that will give you the power to use AI to create, innovate, and shape the future. With these tools and resources at your disposal, you can make a difference and make something really special.

Remember that the journey of AI isn't just about learning and coding; it's also about exploring, learning, and having fun along the way. Accept the challenges, enjoy the wins, and never stop being interested. You have what it takes to become a young expert in AI and leave your mark on the world. So, go ahead and use these tools and resources to get started on your AI adventures. The future is waiting for your brilliant and creative ideas to shape it. AI is a great tool for exploring, learning, and building.

In the next and final chapter, I will quickly summarize what we have learned along our journey so far. I will also discuss what the future of AI could look like. And who knows? You might be the one playing a key role in shaping it!

9

The Future of AI

OUR JOURNEY SO FAR

We have come a long way on our exciting journey into the world of AI. In the previous chapters, we discovered what artificial intelligence is, looked at the different kinds of AI, and learned about its fascinating history. We talked about how AI works and how it affects education and jobs. We also talked about how important ethics are in AI. We discovered new tools and resources we could use to continue our journey of learning. Now that we've come to the end of our trip, let us take a moment to think about what we've learned so far and what the future holds for AI.

During our discussions, we found out that artificial intelligence (AI) is like a superpower that helps computers and robots think, learn, and make decisions. We looked at the different kinds of AI, from narrow AI that helps us with specific tasks to the exciting possibilities of super AI that can do amazing things. We went on a trip through time and learned about some of the most important moments in the history of

AI, from ancient times to the present. We also saw how AI has become an important part of our everyday lives.

We also learned how AI works on the inside, where data, machine learning, and programming are very important. We saw how AI can change education by turning into a helpful learning buddy, a teacher's assistant, and powering the classrooms of the future. We looked into how AI affects jobs and creativity, and we saw how it is changing many jobs while also making us more creative and letting us work with AI as creative partners.

When we talked about ethics, we all agreed that it was important to use AI in a fair and respectful way and make ethical decisions. We talked about how AI could be dangerous, but we also talked about how it needs moral rules to help it develop in a way that will help people.

AI is on the verge of an exciting new era. There are so many options! AI is likely to keep changing our world, helping us deal with global problems and find new things. But it's up to us, the young explorers and future leaders, to make sure AI stays a force for good, creativity, and positive change. So, let's take a moment to celebrate how far we've come and get ready for the exciting future of AI. Together, we can go to new places, make good decisions, and use the full power of Artificial Intelligence.

FUTURE TRENDS

In this final section, I will simply present to you five possible impacts of AI on areas that we have not really talked about so far in the book. I hope it convinces you that the applications of AI are indeed very universal, and we are just scratching the surface in terms of all the possibilities.

Saving Planet Earth

AI has great potential to help people protect the environment and build a more sustainable future. Let's look at some more instances of how AI can promote energy and environmental efficiency:

1. **Protecting Wildlife:** Drones equipped with specialized AI technology can help us monitor animals and defend those who are in danger. These aerial drones have the ability to photograph various landscapes, including forests and oceans. They take pictures that aid in locating and better illuminating animals. We can make wise decisions to keep them safe and safeguard their homes if we have more information about them. Even people who harm animals—such as those who engage in illegal animal hunting—can be apprehended with the aid of these sophisticated drones.

2. **Fighting Climate Change:** As you already know, AI is capable of analyzing images and data from various sources, including satellites and social media posts on Facebook and Twitter. Using these, it can identify hidden patterns and predict future events. Have you heard about the El Nino phenomenon? It is

an undesirable weather pattern linked to climate change that can harm crops, result in floods, and have an impact on fishing. Scientists are now using AI to address the effects of global warming and patterns like El Nino. For example, during floods, AI can provide quick maps to assist in the distribution of emergency resources. It can also help scientists make better predictions on where the effects may be the worst, so that preparations can be made in advance.

3. **Taking Care of Forests:** Our forests, which serve as vital habitats for numerous plants and animals, can be taken care of with the aid of AI. Artificial intelligence (AI) can examine images from space to determine whether excessive tree-cutting is occurring due to illegal logging or mining. Additionally, it can determine the health of the forests and any changes. With this knowledge, we can collaborate to safeguard the forests and ensure their long-term health. AI can even assist us in strategically planting new trees so that more forests can develop.

4. **Smart Farming:** Artificial intelligence (AI) can help with smart farming, which is farming that is environmentally friendly. To determine when to water the plants, it can consider data on the soil, weather, and how the plants are doing. Farmers can use the correct amount of water and prevent waste by using AI. AI can assist farmers in finding more effective pest control methods that don't involve using dangerous chemicals. This keeps the environment secure and the plants healthy. Farmers

can produce more food while protecting the environment with the aid of AI.

5. **Energy Savings:** AI can assist us in reducing the amount of energy we use in buildings like homes and schools. In order to save energy, specialized AI systems can monitor how people use the buildings and modify settings for the lighting and temperature. They can even estimate how much energy we will require and ensure that it is used efficiently. We can use AI to make buildings more environmentally friendly and safeguard the environment.

6. **Waste management and recycling:** Artificial intelligence (AI) has the potential to improve waste management and recycling. When presented with images of various waste types, AI can automatically group them into the appropriate categories. This facilitates recycling and encourages us to reuse items rather than dispose of them. Using AI, the best routes for garbage trucks can be planned, resulting in less fuel consumption and pollution.

Exploring Space

Space has always fascinated humans, and we have already made a lot of progress in understanding our universe. However, AI can take our efforts to the next level. Here are some examples:

1. **Robots in space:** It is possible to send AI-powered robots to distant planets, moons, and asteroids to gather data on them. These robots are very intelligent. They are mobile and can

gather soil and rock samples. To make decisions independently and adapt to unforeseen circumstances, they use specialized AI technology. They then relay critical data to Earth-based scientists.

Exploring New Planets with AI-assisted Rovers

2. The Future of AI AI can be an excellent aid to astronauts during their space missions. AI-enhanced, intelligent robots may resemble their space companions! They help astronauts with important jobs like maintaining the spacecraft, carrying out experiments, and fixing things. These robots' exceptional abilities and capacity for handling difficult tasks ensure the astronauts' safety and the mission's success.

3. **Predicting Space Weather:** AI can assist scientists in making predictions about space weather, such as solar flares and radiation levels. We can better plan space missions and avert hazardous situations by understanding space weather patterns.

In order to keep us safe in space, AI can even provide early warnings about space weather events that might impact communication systems and satellites.

4. **Exoplanet Explorers:** AI can aid in the search for exoplanets, or planets outside of our solar system. They collect a lot of data using large telescopes, which AI algorithms can then analyze. AI can find data patterns that point to the existence of exoplanets. This aids in concentrating research efforts on the most intriguing planets. AI also aids in our understanding of the make-up and unique characteristics of these distant planets.

5. **Space Mission Planning:** AI can assist in the planning of space missions and ensure that spacecraft travel as safely as possible. The force of gravity, the best routes, and the amount of fuel required are all factors that AI algorithms take into account. This aids in more effective mission planning and accurate space navigation. It guarantees that missions are safe and make efficient use of resources.

AI For Assistive Technologies

AI functions as a unique tool that can be incredibly beneficial to people with disabilities. More examples of how AI can empower and assist them are provided below:

1. **Smart Prosthetics:** AI-enabled prosthetic limbs can significantly improve the quality of life for those who have limb differences. These prosthetic limbs have AI technology that

allows them to move more naturally and precisely. With AI, people can more easily control their prosthetic limbs, increasing their mobility and enabling them to carry out daily tasks with increased confidence and independence.

2. **Speech Assistant:** AI can assist those who have trouble speaking by facilitating communication. AI can convert thoughts into words for people who are unable to communicate through voice. Utilizing specialized equipment that can read eye or brain signals, this is accomplished. AI algorithms can translate these signals into spoken words, enabling people to communicate and interact with others effectively. AI algorithms can translate these signals into spoken words, enabling people to communicate and interact with others effectively.

3. **Vision Support:** AI can help those who have vision problems by giving them tools that improve their vision. AI-powered gadgets can assist with reading aloud text, object recognition, and environment description. By providing audio instructions and alerts about obstacles or changes in their surroundings, AI, for instance, can assist a blind person in navigating their environment.

4. **Learning Tools:** AI can also assist students with a variety of learning needs. Learning tools powered by AI can adjust to the skills of each student and offer individualized support. For instance, AI can provide additional explanations or practice

questions as needed, improving everyone's access to and enjoyment of learning.

5. **Accessibility in Daily Life:** By enhancing accessibility in daily life, AI can help build a more inclusive society. AI can assist with tasks like creating user-friendly websites and apps, providing subtitles or translations for videos, or even interpreting sign language. With the help of AI, we can guarantee that everyone has equal access to information, participation in activities, and social inclusion. It will be a change for the better and a great benefit for humanity, indeed.

CONCLUSION

Young explorers, congratulations on finishing this amazing journey into the field of artificial intelligence! We have learned about the marvels of AI, its various subtypes, and the fascinating history of AI. We've learned how AI operates, examined how it affects employment, education, and creativity, and talked about how important ethics are in this fascinating field. We have seen how AI has the potential to create a better future for all of us.

But keep in mind that this is just the start of a huge revolution! We are at the forefront of a world in which artificial intelligence will continue to astound us and change our lives. We are forerunners of a future that is still developing, one in which artificial intelligence (AI) will play a larger role in determining how we learn, work, explore, and interact with others.

Keep in mind that you have the ability to influence change. AI belongs to all of us; it is not just for experts or scientists. The next generation of AI enthusiasts, creators, and innovators could be you. You have the opportunity to take part in the adventure, and the possibilities are endless.

Ask questions, let your curiosity run wild, and keep exploring. Explore the incredible websites, tools, and resources we've provided for you. Dream big, code, and produce! We can create a future where technology and humanity coexist for the good of all if we use AI as our ally.

Recall that moral conduct is essential. Let's continue to put fairness, inclusivity, and respect first as we move forward on this journey. Let's make sure AI is applied for the greater good and to address the problems the world faces.

The amazing AI revolution is still in its early stages. Keep your imagination alive and be open to the opportunities that lie ahead. Let your ideas soar, your voice be heard, and your dreams influence the course of history. You are the protagonists of this thrilling new chapter of the AI adventure, which has just started!

I truly appreciate your participation in this unique journey. May your AI journey be one of wonder, discovery, and limitless potential. If you liked this book, please help me spread the word by:

- Leaving a 5-star review on Amazon. Mention what you loved about the book and how it is inspiring you

- Telling your siblings, classmates, friends and relatives about this book

- Recommending this book to your teacher for use in class, and

- Sharing your thoughts on social media and providing a link to the book to your network

Last but not least, do check out our other titles and stay tuned for new and exciting releases from Lexicon Labs.

I wish you lots of good luck and new adventures!

Dr. Leo Lexicon

More fun titles from Lexicon Labs for all ages!

(Be sure to check Dr. Leo Lexicon's
Author Page on Amazon for new releases)

 @LeoLexicon

LEXICON LABS

9 798223 077978